Do
ADVERTISING CAMPAIGNS...
that insult your intelligence make you

HOPPING MAD?

● ● ●

Do
TELEVISION SHOWS...
written for 6-year-old morons make you

HOPPING MAD?

● ● ●

Do
MOTION PICTURES...
that appeal to sex perverts make you

HO _ _ _ NG MAD?

● ● ●

Do
POLITICIA _ _
helping _ _ _ _ _ _ _ _ _ _ _ _ _ _ _ u

HOPPIN _

● ● ●

Do
ALL THE OTHER CLODS...
bilking, conning, cheating and committing
other crimes against the public make you

HOPPING MAD?

● ● ●

WELL, THEN, *THIS* CRIME AGAINST THE PUBLIC
–THIS "COME-ON PAGE"–OUGHT TO MAKE YOU

"HOPPING MAD"

(Mainly because it's the exact same "Come-On Page"
we ran in our previous collection, "Good 'n' MAD"!)

More MAD Humor from SIGNET

HOPPING MAD

Charles M. Schulz, the creator of "Peanuts" has a warm, happy, secure way of looking at things. In his "Happiness Is A Warm Puppy", he told us about the things in childhood that make us happy. MAD, in the belief that childhood is more miserable than happy, answered Mr. Schulz with its parody, "Misery Is A Cold Hot Dog". Now, Mr. Schulz has another best-seller called, "Security Is A Thumb And A Blanket," which reveals the things in childhood that make us feel secure, like: "Security is having a big brother." and "Security is a candy bar hidden in the freezer." Once again, MAD takes exception. All we remember of childhood are the things that made us feel "INsecure", like . . .

INSECURITY
IS A PAIR OF
LOOSE SWIM TRUNKS

ARTIST: BOB CLARKE   WRITER: FRANK JACOBS

6

**Insecurity is a hole in
both your front pockets.**

**Insecurity is moving into
a new neighborhood.**

**Insecurity is coming home alone
from a horror movie.**

Insecurity is holding a baby.

**Insecurity is bringing a sealed
note home from your teacher.**

Insecurity is sleeping in the upper bunk the first night at camp.

Insecurity is when the ferris wheel stops and you're at the top.

9

Insecurity is being
a tall 11-year-old.

Insecurity is being the odd
kid in a choose-up game.

10

Insecurity is your sister getting
chicken pox before Christmas
vacation, and you never had it.

Insecurity is having a father
who's an accountant.

Insecurity is eating something 11
with a big dog watching.

**Insecurity is when they start
surveying your favorite vacant lot.**

**Insecurity is being the last
to hand in a test paper.**

Insecurity is going by yourself
for the first time.

Insecurity is waiting for the
thermometer to come out.

13

Insecurity is going downtown
and seeing two Santa Clauses.

Insecurity is a tough kid
approaching your sand castle.

**Insecurity is your mother and
father arguing downstairs.**

**Insecurity is your ball
bouncing into traffic.**

**Insecurity is running an
errand with a 10-dollar bill.**

**Insecurity is trying not to
look guilty when accused of
something you didn't do.**

**Insecurity is going into
a strange store with
a deposit bottle.**

**Insecurity is examining
a fire cracker that
didn't go off.**

**Insecurity is
a helium-filled balloon.**

**Insecurity is being the first
to hand in a test paper.**

THE MALADY LINGERS ON DEPT.

In recent years, scholars have been frittering away more and more time, trying to learn how our present-day forms of popular music evolved from the different rhythms and structures of the past. In the course of their studies, they've stumbled across the startling fact that many of today's biggest hits aren't really new tunes at all, but are actually modernized versions of earlier classics. Well, if MAD had had any scholars on its staff, it might've added meaningful data to this fascinating discovery. However, by being forced to make do with only the idiots available, we were merely able to bungle our way through this attempt to trace . . .

THE
EVOLUTION
OF A
POPULAR
SONG

ARTIST: GEORGE WOODBRIDGE   WRITER: TOM KOCH

I

Like so many of today's "smash hits," the selection MAD traced first saw the light of day in early England where the downtrodden dolt sought to lighten his burden by lifting his voice in song. The original composer is unknown, except for indications that his name was "Anonymous." It has been substantiated that the song enjoyed wide popularity after it was adopted as a theme by the Four Churls:

Me Loche 'N Beastie

When Aye gae to sae mae killy kairn,
'Tis the fol' o' dew a charnie bairn;
Tu lookie, tu loodie, tu wipple;
An' the auld man flipt an' diede.

II

Naturally, the incessant repetition of this chanty forced otherwise docile English peasants to flee the country and seek a new and better life in America. Bringing their music with them, they soon discovered that the song under study made even less sense over here than it had back at home. So it was revised to blend in with the new surroundings, and thus became the first-known American Folk Song:

The Yokel's Lament

My true love, Emmie, lives up on the hill;
Tu loodie, tu loodie, tu lai.
My true love, Emmie, lives up on the hill,
But I can't go to court her 'cause
    it's too far to walk,
And the mule is sick,
So I think I'll find me a pretty little girl
    in the valley 'cause it's downhill all the way;
Tu loodie, tu loodie, tu wipple.

III

Though the song had been converted into the more familiar "love ballad" form, the retention of the meaningless "tu loodie, tu loodie" business called for further revisions to cope with the ever-changing times. Thus, when it next cropped up during the Civil War, it had become an inspirational marching song for the fighting men of the South:

The Battle Hymn Of The Confederacy

Oh, we're gwyna hang mah true love
    from a sour apple tree;
Then we're gwyna all dance 'round her
    and we'll holler loud with glee;
But we'd best get goin' soon
    or thar won't be no time, you see:
We're gwyna lose the war!

    Glory, glory, Emmie Botsford.
    Glory, glory, Emmie Botsford.
    Glory, glory, Emmie Botsford.
        Her feet go stumblin' on!

IV

ith the ending of the Civil War, the bottom mysteriously
opped out of the marching song market, and in the dark
ys of the Reconstruction Era that followed, inspiring tunes
battle gave way to the more mournful laments of work
ngs and chain gangs:

Nobody Knows
The Bollix I've Made

Nobody knows the bollix I've made;
Nobody knows my bungle.
Nobody knows the bollix I've made;
Why did I trust Emmie?

She was my love through thick and through thin;
Then she turned fink against me.
When I get hold of Emmie agin'—
Scream! Eccch! Hallelujah!

V

And it required only a short step for the prison lament to evolve into the mournful blues that echoed along the Mississippi River before the turn of the century. Quite naturally, the song under study remained alive, only with minor but significant changes through the period:

I Got A Right
To Rub Her Out

I got a right to rub her out;
She's got a right to moan and sigh;
I got a right to wave bye-bye,
And dump her in the river.

She was my true love, Emmie Lou;
I thought she walked with style and grace.
But anyone with such a face
Belongs down in the river.

VI

But such earthy lyrics could scarcely be expected to find acceptance in those genteel, conservative drawing rooms of the early 1900's, And so once again, the song underwent a revamping in order to gain new approval and enjoy a new surge of popularity . . .

Go, Little Emmie

Go, little Emmie, quickly, quickly;
When you are near, I'm sickly, sickly;
Go to Seattle, Butte or Nutley;
I don't care where, but leave abruptly;
Please hop a freight, be it fast or slow;
But go, little Emmie, go.

VII

With the outbreak of World War I, many things changed in America, including the music. Men like Irving Berlin and George M. Cohan set the pace, and vibrant patriotic tunes suddenly came into vogue. Somehow, the song under study managed to survive—with a little fixing here and there:

You're A Fat Old Hag

You're a fat old hag,
   You're an unsightly bag,
But you're still my true love, Emmie Lou;
   You're the emblem of
The land I love;
   Your complexion is red, white and blue.
Overweight and big
   In your ill-fitting wig,
Oh, forever in peace may it wag;
   And should old acquaintance be forgot,
I'll escape from that fat old hag.

VIII

Came the roaring twenties, and jazz burst forth from New Orleans to engulf the nation. Song writers, hard-pressed to meet the musical demands of the era, dug back into the sure-fire repertoires of the past to find their jazz-age inspirations. And so the tune under study was modified:

Bye-Bye, Emmie

Pack up all your clothes and junk;
Fill your grip and steamer trunk;
    Bye-bye, Emmie!
Go to Flint or Battle Creek;
Just don't stay, that's all I seek;
    Bye-bye, Emmie!
No one here can stand or comprehend you;
That's the reason we all want to send you;
Lock the door, turn out the light;
Then take off by late tonight;
    Emmie, bye-bye!

IX

Maybe it was the general lethargy of the Depression; maybe it was the coming of those gosh-awful movie musicals—whatever it was, it had to be something pretty ghastly to do what it did to song-writers of the era. Miraculously, our melody came through the horror of it all with no more a mangle job than what the public taste then demanded . . .

Moon Over Sioux City

Moon over Sioux City,
Shine on my Emmie Lou;
  In June I swoon,
  Just like a goon,
When I croon for you.

Moon over Sioux City,
Why won't you dim your light?
  Your glaring beam
Just makes me scream,
  'Cause it's too bright
To sleep
At night!

X

As the nation belatedly was to learn, the ending of World War II had an unexplained tendency to drive the younger people of the U.S. stark staring mad. There seems to be no other explanation for the birth of Rock 'n' Roll. This catastrophe called for a major overhaul to keep our song alive and it was done as masterfully as could be expected:

I'm So Cruel

I know she can be found
Hidin' beneath her couch;
She knows I'm on the prowl
That's why she's in that crouch;
    I'm so cruel!
And Emmie Lou's a fool.

She's
Got lots of other loves,
But I'm the only one she's frightened of.
    Be a pal;
Help me kill my gal!

XI

In defiance of all logic, Rock 'n' Roll is still with us. But its hold on the nation's youth is weakening. In coffee houses and similar dens of the spiritually pooped, a new generation nurtures an even stranger style of music. Whether these weird avant garde rhythms of the coffee houses will ever be understood by the general public, and whether the centuries-old song under study can survive this most radical of changes, only time will tell. But this is what the "beatniks" have done to it in their frenzied effort to produce something that is new and different . . .

Infinity's Five
Dimensions Of Nowhere

When Aye gae to sae mae killy kairn,
'Tis the fol' o' dew a charnie bairn;
Tu lookie, tu loodie, tu wipple;
An' the auld man flipt an' diede.

THE
LIGHTER
SIDE OF

MARRIED
MEN

WRITER & ARTIST: DAVID BERG

Don't you ever do **anything** right? Must I do **everything** around here?!

Don't you ever do **anything** right? Must I do **everything** around here?!

What's with the **hair curlers?!** When I come home, I want my wife to look like a **woman**, not like a **radar antenna!**

But I've **got to** put my hair in curlers so it will **look nice—**

For who? For some **stranger** we might see tonight? How about looking nice for **me** for a change!?

If **that's** the way he wants it, I'll comb out my hair and put on a new dress and **look nice** for **him** at supper!

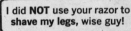

CHOCOLATE SPRINKLES? ESKIMO PIE SANDWICHES? HYDROX COOKIES? MINT JELLY? MALTED BALLS? GOOBERS? MALLOMARS? HERSHEY KISSES? LADY FINGERS? EGG ROLLS? FROZEN PIZZA?

CAN I HAVE SOME MONEY? I'VE GOT TO GO SHOPPING FOR SOME **FOOD**!!

43

44

46

Ever since the first atomic bomb was exploded, the world has lived in mortal fear of nuclear annihilation. Well, we've got news for you! If the bomb don't destroy us first, something even more horrible will! We're referring to the deadliest scourge of all . . . "Junk Mail"—those circulars, form-letters and pamphlets that fill our mail boxes daily, gradually smothering us with their paralyzingly dull contents. Yes, MAD believes that the time has come for Mankind to strike back . . . before it's too late. Here, then, is

THE
MAD
PLAN
FOR FIGHTING THE WAR AGAINST
JUNK MAIL

ARTIST: BOB CLARKE   WRITER: LARRY SIEGEL

THE FIGHT FIRE WITH FIRE

This method works most effectively when you've received a tear-jerking letter from an obviously phony charity organization . . . or even from an obnoxious legitimate one . . . asking for a donation. Like this, for example:

The National Athlete's Feet Foundation

BOX 143   FUNGUS, NORTH DAKOTA

*"Give Generously, So That Others May Walk
Without Itching Something Awful"*

Dear Friend:

Well, here it is--almost Arbor Day again, and time for our Annual Drive to collect funds so that we can continue our fight against one of mankind's most dreaded afflictions--Athlete's Foot. Have you ever seen a child with Athlete's Foot? It's not a pretty sight. Have you ever seen an adult with Athlete's Foot? It's even messier. Wouldn't you like to bring a fresh sparkle to their tired eyes, a bright smile to their wan lips, and a healthy glow to the spaces between their toes?

Thanks to donations in the past from thousands of kind and generous Americans like yourself, we are rapidly approaching the day when Athlete's Foot will be forever wiped from the feet of the earth. Already our competent staff of medical research experts has initiated a dramatic breakthrough in this fight. We have discovered that Athlete's Foot (or Shreddus Gunkus) is not limited to athletes. Anybody can get it! Even you!! But why waste time on involved laboratory terminology designed to scare you. There is still a great deal of ground to cover, and time is growing short.

On Arbor Day, we will stage our Annual "Athlete's Foot Sufferers' March on Washington". Your generous check can aid immeasurably in financing this worthy procession. Remember, we stage only one annual donations drive each Arbor Day. So help us make this year's drive an even bigger one than our one annual drive last Groundhog Day, or our one annual drive last Shrove Tue~~day, o~~ ~~our one annual drive last~~ Simcath

APPROACH

All you do is send a letter like this in reply, and we assure you that you'll never hear from them again!

Gentlemen:

All I can say is "Thank Heavens!" Thank Heavens there are wonderful organizations like yours around to bring Athlete's Foot out into the open, instead of having it discussed behind closed doors as it has been in the past.

Take me, for example, I've had Athlete's Foot for years, but I was afraid to talk about it. Now I'm no longer afraid. I realize that at last I have someone to discuss it with—someone who will sympathize with my terrible problem.

You think your people got Athlete's Foot? Believe me, they don't know what Athlete's Foot is! Now, I've got Athlete's Foot. I've not only got it on my feet, I've got it on my hands—between my fingers! Yes, I've got Athlete's Hand!

And as long as we're discussing interesting physical ailments, I've also got this gnawing pain in my chest when I get up in the morning. Well, it's not really in my chest, it's more like near my stomach, but it starts like in my knee. It doesn't really hurt all the time—just when I breathe.

Of course it's not nearly as bad as this terrible throbbing I get in the bridge of my nose every time I eat ice cream or drink something cold. Wowee! You talk about pain!

Ordinarily, I'm not the type of person who complains, but it isn't often I can find a sympathetic ear.

Let me tell you how it all began. (Besides, it will help me take my mind off these dizzy spells I always get whenever I write letters.)

About six years ago, I suddenly came down with a rare tropical disease, unheard of in this part of

HOW TO HANDLE THOSE

One of the sneakier tricks used by Junk Mailers is their attempt at putting you under an obligation to them. This is done by sending you something of minor value, like . . .

The Reader's Digress
MISERABLEVILLE, N. Y.

Dear Friend:

    Enclosed is a shiny new penny. You are now indebted to us for life, and you would be the world's biggest ingrate if you didn't take out a subscription to the Reader's Digress.
    Now you can learn what's going on in the world by reading our condensed versions of

Another gimmick used by Junk Mailers to put you under an obligation to them is to send samples of their products:

THE
SICK
RAZOR COMPANY
BOX 542
OGLETHORPE,
MICHIGAN

Dear Friend,

    Enclosed is a free sample of our new stainless steel razor blade. This new blade is so sharp that all 322 of our male employees have already shaved with the very same blade that we are sending you, and yet there are still at least 63 shaves left in it.
    Since we have been kind enough to send you this wonderful free gift, you would have to be a real fink not to become one of our steady customers and make regular

TRICKY ENCLOSURES

You'll have the last laugh on Junk Mailers who send you pennies if you send a letter of reply like the following:

Gentlemen:

I would like to take this opportunity to thank you for the rare penny you sent me last week. The "E", the "R" and the "T" in LIBERTY were upside down, and Lincoln was clean shaven.

I have just sold the penny to a coin collector for $40,000, and I am now so wealthy that I can afford to buy all the original publications from which you condense your articles, so you can see that I really do not need a subscription to your magazine which I think is

But a letter of reply like this will create quite a stir:

Gentlemen:

Unfortunately, when sending me that sample of your new stainless steel blade, somebody neglected to close the box in which the blade was enclosed. Your new blade certainly is sharp. So sharp, in fact, that when delivering it to me, my postman accidentally severed his pinky with it.

Now, my postman is planning to institute a negligence suit for $375,000, and he wants to know who is responsible for the accident — you or I. So would you please check through your files to see if I formally requested the sample blade, or if you people just took it upon yourselves to send it to me without even asking

And then there's the insidious method Junk Mailers use to extract information they need—by making you feel guilty for accepting something that you don't even need or want:

There's only one way to keep this Junk Mailer from hounding you. Send the information in a letter like this one:

Metropolis Life Insurance Company

111 BROADWAY, NEW YORK, N.Y.

Dear Friend:—

Enclosed is one of our typical calendars which you didn't request and have no use for, since you've probably received 150 other calendars like it from 150 other insurance companies like ours.

However, since we did give you something for nothing, the least you can do is to thank us by sending us the date of your birth. Then we can really go to work on you, trying to sell our fantastically low rate life insurance policy to you, which you need about as much as you needed the calendar which it was our pleasure to

---

Dear Sirs:

Thank you for the wonderful calendar which you sent to my home. It was forwarded to me here at Sunnydale General Hospital, and I can't tell you how many hours of pleasure I've gotten thumbing through it.

It is awfully nice of you to want to go through the trouble of sending me a fantastically low-rate life insurance policy. I would be delighted to learn the facts. As one who has been given no more than three weeks to live, I welcome any form of diversion which can take my mind off my troubles. At any rate, my date of birth is

WHAT TO DO ABOUT THOSE ANNOYING "FREE TRIAL" OFFERS

Enclosed find sample swatches of Tuttletaub's new "Miracle Tuxedo for Evening Wear". Choose the shade that you want, send us your suit size, and we'll send you a **Tuttletaub Miracle Tux.** Wear it for **10 days.** If you are not completely **satisfied** with it, you may return it **AND PAY NOTHING! THAT'S RIGHT!** Pay no money for the next three weeks and if

NOW...YOURS FREE! TO ENJOY AGAIN AND AGAIN AND AGAIN...! FOR 14 FULL DAYS! *A Brand New*

FORBLEFARB

Combination Washer-Dryer-Air Conditioner-Heater-Power Mower-Can-Opener-Baby-Sitter Walkie-Talkie!

If this isn't the most exciting appliance you've ever owned, you may return it to us and

PAY NO MONEY!

Order your brand new stereophonic, three-dimensional 60-inch RCE Color TV set today! Keep it for 30 days! If you're not delighted with it, return it to us at NO CHARGE! Now, can anything be simpler? Just fill out the coupon

53

There's only one way to stop these pests from bothering you in the future! What you do is **ABUSE THOSE FREE TRIAL OFFERS TO DEATH!** Yes, accept every free trial offer they send you . . . like this "In-The-Know" family:

Bernice, I've decided that I'm not satisfied with my Tuttletaub Miracle Tuxedo. Since my 10-day free trial period is up on Wednesday, I'll return the tux and pick up some Glugg Scuba Diving Gear for a two-week trial period. That should be fun wearing when I'm cleaning out the garage . . .

I think I'll return my Free Trial Moskowitz Mink Stole, too, Herman! It sorts of pulls on my shoulders when I bend over to pick up the garbage pail . . .!

I got a pick-up order for 8 free trial TV sets, an air-conditioner, 27 sets of encyclopedias, 150 books, 19 stereo sets and a garbage disposal unit—which you are returning. Where do you want my men to install your 30-day free-trial Minchwell Swimming Pool?

55

Chances are you receive Junk Mail like this quite often

Dear Friend:-
This is a chain letter. It was started by a
man like yourself in hopes that it might
bring relief and happiness to tired business-
men. Unlike most chain letters, this one does
not involve money. Simply send a copy of this
letter to three of your friends who are
equally tired. Then, bundle up your wife and
send her to the man whose name is at the top
of the list, and add your name to the bottom.
When your name comes to the top of the list,
you will have received 4,789 women--and some
of them will be dandies. Have faith. Do not
break the chain! One man _did_, and he got his
own wife back!

Arnold Mednicov
230 Vladin Street,
Canton, Ohio

Daniel Frumm
45 Yorkel Avenue
Takoma, Washington

Elbert Glommp
601 Herkimer Drive
Hobart, Texas.

MISCHIEF APPROACH

As you may know, sending chain letters through the mail is illegal. So what you do is make two more exact copies of the chain letter you received. Then, making sure you do not include your name and address anywhere, send one copy of the letter to each of your 3 following friends:

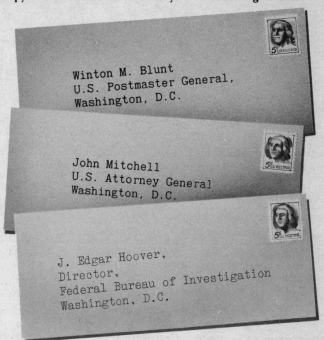

Winton M. Blunt
U.S. Postmaster General,
Washington, D.C.

John Mitchell
U.S. Attorney General
Washington, D.C.

J. Edgar Hoover,
Director,
Federal Bureau of Investigation
Washington, D.C.

Photo Re-Touchers

Here's another example of Junk Mail you may have received:

Dear Friend:—

Do you have any battered photographs of yourself or your loved ones which you'd like touched-up and restored? Also, are there any other people in the photograph whom you'd like erased so that only you or your loved one remains in the picture alone?

We have an exciting MONEY-BACK GUARANTEED offer which we'd like to make. Just

BEFORE

AFTER

What you do is get hold of an old news photo of Coney Island on July 4th, and send it along with this letter:

Gentlemen:

Here is an old photograph which has great sentimental value for me. My beloved Uncle Sigmund is in the 219,426th row up, 3487 people from the left (not counting the ice cream vendor). You can't miss Uncle Sigmund. He's wearing a bathing suit. Kindly erase the other 1,326,287 people and make me a clean 8 × 10 blow up of my Uncle. If I am satisfied, I'll be happy to send you

AT THE MASK STORE

ONE MORNING

THE NEXT AFTERNOON

THE SHOPLIFTER

Drive the all-new, vastly improved, slightly enlarged, basically unchanged, exactly the same as last year...

1964 PLYMUC

The Luxury Car

With The Economy Price

ONLY $2134*

*POWER STEERING, POWER BRAKES, WHITEWALLS, RADIO, HEATER, DEFROSTER, SEATS, ROOF, FLOOR, FRAME, PAINT JOB, AND DELIVERY BEYOND FACTORY GATE OPTIONAL AT EXTRA COST.

The two ads above are typical of hundreds you've seen before. Notice anything about them to make you snarl, stamp your feet, jump up and down and scream in anger? We're talking about that little asterisk next to the price! We've all been conditioned to *accept* this sneaky little trick in ads for *high-priced items!* And this could prove to be our undoing. Because manufacturers of *low-priced items* will take courage and adopt this nefarious practice and we'll be seeing ads like the following, in which we'll have to be especially careful to

WATCH THAT PRICE WITH THE ASTERISK*

*MAINLY BECAUSE A SNEAKY LOW PRICE CAN BECOME A RIDICULOUS HIGH PRICE AT BUYING TIME!

ARTIST: BOB CLARKE   WRITER: AL JAFFEE

SPECIAL SALE

only

$2 98 *

THE FABULOUS SUNBEAM STEAM-AND-DRY IRON

* PLUS HANDLING CHARGE

The "Handling Charge" in this case means the charge for putting on the handle. Without a handle, a 450° iron is very hard to—er—handle. The extra $12 charge is worth it considering the advantage of not burning your hands.

GREENTHUM NURSERY'S
BARGAIN-OF-THE-MONTH

4 FOOT EVERGREENS
$4⁰⁰*
EACH

*AS SHOWN

Note that these evergreens "As Shown" have no roots, as this is "Bargain-Of-The-Month" for January! Which means these are unsold Christmas Tree evergreens, soon to turn ever*browns!* Four-foot evergreen *with roots* is $15 extra.

SHOE KING IRVING
slashes prices *IN HALF!*

MEN'S SHOES
FORMERLY $10 A PAIR

$5⁰⁰*

ALL SIZES

* EACH

That's right! At $5.00 *each,* a pair of these shoes will cost the same as they cost before—$10. See how you're catching on? Now, you'll always remember to watch the *!

BULBS

7¢*

EACH

*ANY LEFT IN STOCK

"Any Left In Stock" refers to any bulbs with *left-hand thread* in stock! If you happen to find any, and you have sockets with left-hand thread, you're in! The rest of us will have to pay 31¢ for regular right-hand thread bulbs.

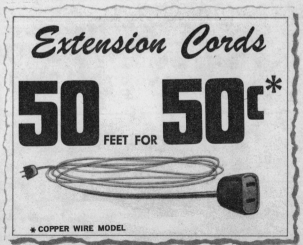

Extension Cords

50 FEET FOR **50c***

* COPPER WIRE MODEL

"Copper Wire Model" means exactly that, and actually does cost 50¢. However, most folks prefer *"Insulated* Copper Wire Model", offering less shock hazard, costing $1.98.

71

TOP QUALITY MONGROL PENCILS

1¢* EACH

*LEAD OPTIONAL AT EXTRA COST

Since lead is 14¢ extra, pencil that writes is actually no bargain. Naturally, some trouble-making malcontents will insist on getting 1¢ pencils, so dealer is prepared with ample stock of solid wood ones just for this purpose.

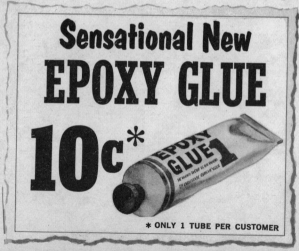

Sensational New EPOXY GLUE

10¢*

* ONLY 1 TUBE PER CUSTOMER

"Only One Tube Per Customer" means you only get #1 tube! But it so happens that epoxy glue is useless unless mixed with hardener—which comes in #2 tube, and costs 98¢.

SIZZLING, DELICIOUS
LARGE PIZZA

49 EACH

*TO GO ONLY

If eaten in Pizza Parlor, pie costs regular $1.50. Clever "To Go" price of 49¢ does not include cardboard carton which costs $1.01. Anyone who has ever carried hot, gooey pizza in his bare hands will gladly pay price of carton.

BEAUTIFUL-PRACTICAL-LONG LASTING
ARMSTUNG FLOORING
at a NEW LOW PRICE!

2c *per tile**

* FOR EXACT SIZE ILLUSTRATED

Using tiles the size of the one illustrated, the average room would require 5000 tiles, and cost $100. Regular 9x9's would do same job in one quarter the time for $37.

A MAD

LOOK
AT
THE
CIRCUS

ARTIST & WRITER: SERGIO ARAGONES

BOOM !

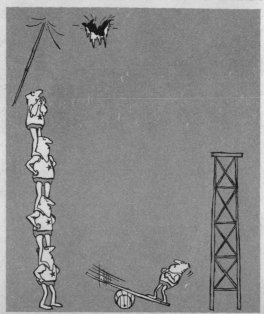

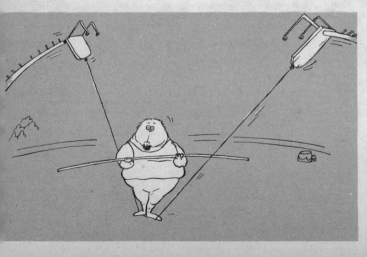

89

Manufacturers originally introduced filters on cigarettes for ladies who were squeamish about known side effects like nicotine stains on the teeth. Today, manufacturers are ballyhooing filters on cigarettes for people who are squeamish about known side effects like cancer of the lungs. And there's a lot of competition among these manufacturers as to whose filter does the better job. In fact, right now, we're witnessing

THE GREAT
FILTER TIP
CIGARETTE

ARTIST: BOB CLARKE   WRITER: AL JAFFEE   91

BATTLE CRIES OF MODERN

Maker claims that his filter helps eliminate the common irritation: "Nicotine-stain mouth."

Maker claims that his filter helps eliminate the annoying condition: "Tar-and-resin throat."

FILTER CIGARETTES

BRAND "C"

Maker claims that his filter helps eliminate the sickening illness: "Inflamed esophagus."

BRAND "D"

Maker claims that his filter helps stop the disgusting affliction: "Laceration of lungs."

BRAND "X"

Maker claims that his going out of business helps stop them other awful smoking hazards.

Filter tip cigarette ads reveal one clear fact: there's a lot of terrible stuff in them cigarettes to filter out! But that's no more reason to give up smoking than for a pearl diver to give up diving — just because a few sharks are lurking around. The diver can depend on his trusty knife . . . and the smoker can depend on his trusty filter.

93

SOME HEALTH-SAVING

KENT'S
MICRONITE FILTER

MARLBORO'S
SELECTRATE FILTER

This filter claims to contain "balancing" mechanism which ingeniously measures correct amount of flavor and irritants it lets thru.

This filter claims to be a "selective" one — allowing the friendly smiling flavor to pass thru, and rejecting the anti-social irritants.

SOME HEALTH-SAVING

MOCK FILTER

SECRET FILTER

Inhaling lit filter is much worse than inhaling lit cigarette. This filter is "all tobacco" . . . for people who always light the wrong end.

Since some he-men feel it's sissy to smoke a cigarette with a filter, this one is secretly hidden inside one end of a straight cigarette.

FILTERS NOW IN USE

TAREYTON'S
DUAL FILTER

This filter contains "dual" elements — a pure white unit working beside an activated charcoal one to deliver new integrated smoking pleasure.

LARK'S
3-PIECE KEITH FILTER

This filter, which contains 3 units — 1 charcoal granule unit between 2 regular pure white units — paves way for future filtration idiocies.

FILTERS COMING SOON

"LITMUS" FILTER

This filter changes color chemically, corresponding to changes in condition of throat and lungs, thus discourages excessive smoking.

SWELL FILTER

This ingenious filter uses highly absorbent blotting paper which swells up from smoker's saliva, clogs up cigarette end, stops smoke.

KING SIZE FILTER

This new "King Size" filter is 90% effective because 90% of the cigarette is filter. This cuts out 90% of the hazards of smoking.

EXPEL-O-FILTER

Inhaling brings the smoke into this new filter where its spring-powered plunger pushes it right back out — and no smoke is good smoke!

NOISE-MAKER FILTER

Inhaling on this new filter causes pitiful wheezing and gasping effect like victim of asthma produces—a sound way to cut down on smoking.

FILTER FILTER

This new filter filters out the harsh irritants usually found in filters. Snaps on easily — paves way for most idiotic filtration idea yet.

DD-A-FILTER CIGARETTES
N IDEA FOR ENDING THE GREAT FILTER-TIP WAR

The "Add-a-Filter Cigarette" makes all other filter-tip cigarettes obsolete. Not only does it protect the flavor, your health, and the American way of life . . . but it adds even more! Mainly another page to this ridiculous article.

Seriously, an "Add-a-Filter Cigarette" not only protects, it medicates. Each filter contains an atomized extract of a drug which is then gently wafted through the smoker's innards to form a protective film over his vital organs.

WHAT IS "ADD-A-FILTER"?

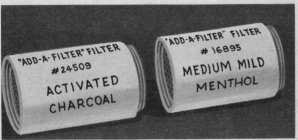

"Add-a-Filter" filter tips are threaded — male at one end, female at the other — so that one or more can be combined.

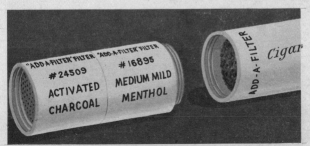

"Add-a-Filter Cigarette" has threaded end to accommodate one — two — or any amount of custom-selected filter tips.

97

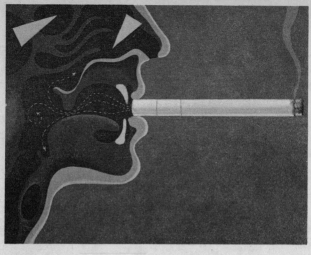

Smoke travels through combination of filters, picks up medications, spreads blessed relief, heals deteriorating tissues, membranes, and other (*yecch*) things like that.

"ADD-A-FILTERS" AVAILABLE

Penicillin	Cortisone	Neo Synephrine
Dramamine	Listerine	Absorbine
Bakedbean	Fluoristan	Krebiozen
Aureomycin	Tetramycin	Lanvinsmycin
Metrecal	Nair	Silicare
G.L.-70	Midol	Miltown
Tums	Vicks	Menthol

Above is partial list of "Add-a-Filters" available which treat every internal organ of body affected by smoking. Remember, smoke travels medicine further — *and* it is mild.

"ADD-A-FILTER CIGARETTE" IN USE...

King Size Kent

Smoker of "Add-a-Filter" is completely relaxed, secure in the knowledge that not only are disease-causing irritants being filtered OUT, but his minimum daily requirement of every medication known to science is being filtered IN!

DON
MARTIN
IN AN

ITALIAN
RESTAURANT

103

SCHKLURT

109

STARS IN YOUR BUYS DEPT.

Watch yourself at all times! Especially if you're an LP record collector! Because the competition in the record album business is pretty keen and some sneaky tricks are being pulled by a few

FAKE
RECORD

ARTIST: JACK RICKARD

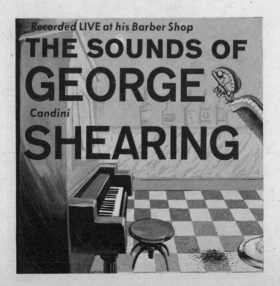

110

small but crafty recording companies. Mainly, the titles of their albums don't always tell exactly who—or what— is on the record inside the jacket! You'll see what we mean as you study these...

-OUT JACKETS

WRITERS: JIM & DARLENE RUTHERFORD

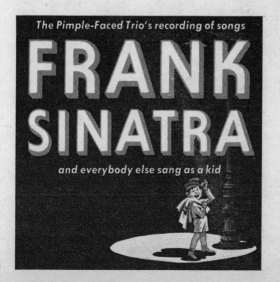

The Pimple-Faced Trio's recording of songs

FRANK SINATRA

and everybody else sang as a kid

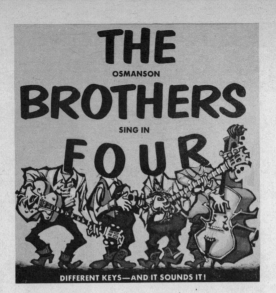

THE
OSMANSON
BROTHERS
SING IN
FOUR

DIFFERENT KEYS—AND IT SOUNDS IT!

LESTER
KALLAKAK SINGS
FLATT
ON THIS RECORD OF POLISH
FOLK
SONGS

ONLY THE PARENTS OF THE KIDS CAN STAND

The Sound Of Music

played by the Potrzebie High School Orchestra

Julie LIPSCHITZ AT THE London AIRPORT

THE ORIGINAL CAST
refused to appear at this recording of music from

Camelot

because we wouldn't pay scale

ON STRIKE   STRIKE   STRIKE   ON STRIKE   STRIKE

THE people of *KINGSTON* N.Y. hate this *TRIO* called "The Incoherents"

HARRY BELAFONTE
COMPLETELY IGNORED THESE TERRIBLE
CALYPSO SONGS

the BIG BAND of
BILLY MAZELTOV MAY
SOUND BETTER SOMEDAY, SO WE GRABBED THIS RECORDING
AT A LOW PRICE WHILE WE HAD THE CHANCE

CORPSE AND ROBBERS DEPT.

Okay, Gang! It's time for another MAD version of a popular movie. Lean back, relax, take your shoes off, notice that the people sitting next to you are running for other seats, put your shoes back on, and join us as

MAD VISITS THE PRODUCER-DIRECTOR OF

"CHARADES"

ARTIST: MORT DRUCKER   WRITER: LARRY SIEGEL

Hello, there! I'm Stanley Done-In, the Producer-Director of the film "CHARADES"! I'd like to show you—Hey! Stop the projector! Have you gone out of your mind?!
What's the matter, S.D.? Aren't the opening titles modernistic enough? Isn't the opening musical score jazzy enough?
They're both fine—but who starts a movie nowadays with opening titles? First you get in drama—then plot-development—then the climax—then the words "The End" . . . THEN the opening titles! !
CARY GRAND and AUDREY HEARTBURN
play
"CHARADES"

There—that's a much better opening... a dead body being thrown from a train!

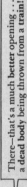

In a horrible comedy like this—I mean a horror-comedy like this, you must shock the audience immediately...

This may come as a shock to **Mr. Done-In,** but I'm not a dead body! We commuters on the Long Island Railroad always get tossed off the train at our stops like this!

The dead body was gently lifted off a mile back!

118

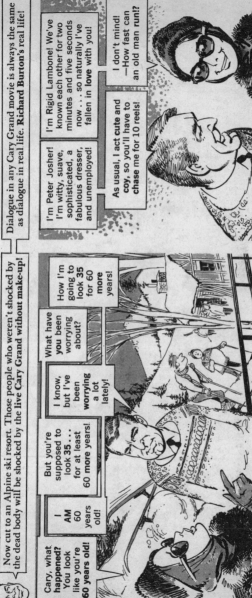

119

Injecting humor into morbid scenes is a prerequisite of a horror-comedy like this one. Take this scene at the funeral, where we meet three murder suspects:

I'm Leopold Giddyman! I'm sneezing in the corpse's face to see if he's really dead!

I'm Kentuck Pentup! I'm pushing a mirror under the corpse's nose . . . to see if he's really dead!

I'm Herman Scuba! I'm sticking a pin into the corpse's hand to see if he's really dead!

Well, the way you three all stormed in here, if he was faking up to now, you probably scared him to death!

Now we cut to the exciting suspense-filled scene when Rigid arrives at her apartment in Paris and finds it stripped bare. She rushes from room to room opening closets—

What a shock! What an awful disappointment! You must feel terrible not finding any clothes in your closets!

I don't feel half as bad as the audience! They're shocked and disappointed because I didn't find any bodies in my closets!

Note the injection of humor in this next gripping scene of intrigue at the U.S. Embassy...

Next, the hero takes the heroine to a Paris night club, and being so debonnair and sophisticated, they naturally play "pass the orange" on the dance floor.

What's this got to do with the plot?

Not a thing! It just gives me a chance to act cute and coy with this fat lady—so all the fat ladies in the audience can identify with her!

...so anyway, your husband was murdered and his body thrown from that train. The three main suspects are old army buddies of his. They're after $250,000 the four of them stole from the U.S. Government during the war. Your husband is believed to have hidden it somewhere...

Why is a distinguished Ambassador like you telling me this horrible news while wearing those ridiculous shorts?

The writer couldn't think of any witty remarks I could make to get laughs!

And then, a hysterical **new** development! The hero, Peter Josher, becomes a fourth suspect!

Scuba just phoned to tell me you're not really Peter Josher—and that **you're** after the money too!

That's **right!** Now the plot starts to get **complicated!** You see, for the rest of the movie, I'll pretend to be **many different people!** That's why the picture is called "**Charades**"! Get it?

The third suspect, Scuba—a big, fat, grotesque slobbering hulk with an artificial hand—waits for Rigid and threatens her in her hotel room.

You better meet me with the money in front of Notre Dame Cathedral tomorrow at noon— **O R E L S E ! !**

How will I be able to recognize you?

I'll wear a rose in my lapel!

Now for the scene that's a "must" for every horror-comedy movie like this one—the thrilling but frightening fight on the rooftop—with witty remarks to take the edge off—

You know what I'm going to do with you? I'm going to rip out your eyes and throw you off the roof and you'll hit the ground and smash all your bones and bleed all over the . . .

Gee whiz, Scuba . . . can't you ever be serious!?

F'rinstance, now that I'm no longer Peter Josher, I'll be Alex Dial! And when you find out I'm not Alex Dial, I'll be Adam Caulfield . . . then Mike Stokie . . . then Hans Conried . . .

Well, after you pretend to be all those people, who will you turn out to be—really and truly?

Let's save that for the big climax scene! Meanwhile, just to inject a serious note into all this hilarious horror . . . . . . I'm taking a shower with all my clothes on!

And finally, Kentuck is found with a vinyl plastic bag tied over his head.

How's this?—'Obviously the murderer didn't want to let the cat out of the **BAG!**'

Better still—'That **WRAPS UP** the last of the suspects!' ... which means I'm in plenty trouble!

Next, Giddyman's throat is slit in an elevator . . .

I got one—'Looks like somebody gave him the **SHAFT!**'

Not bad! Here's a better one!—'The murderer really showed him **WHERE TO GET OFF!**'

And now for some really funny scenes: Scuba is found drowned in a bathtub.

This calls for some witty bathtub remark! How about: 'Too bad he died before he had a chance to **COME CLEAN!**'

That's clever! How about: 'This crime has a familiar **RING** to it!'

It was used before in "Man On The Eiffel Tower"!

How's this place for a climax?

I know that! But our big climax takes place in that French theatre we just passed!

A theater!? What a dull place for an exciting climax scene! Keep running!

Why are you running away from me, Rigid?

Because no more suspects leaves only YOU! Besides, in horror-comedies, there's always a big chase leading to a fantastic climax scene at a world-famous geographical landmark!

127

129

Anyway, that's "Charades"—folks! A picture full of murder, suspense, shock, chases, tongue-in-cheek dialogue and sex! Which brings us to another surprise! I'm really playing Charades myself! You see—I'm not really Stanley Done-In!

I'm really ALFRED HATCHPLOT! Who else could've made this picture?

Then if you're Doris Daye . . . The murderer must be . . .

STOP THE PROJECTOR! THAT'S ENOUGH! LET'S NOT GIVE AWAY THE BIG SURPRISE! ! !

ike other forms of life, Primitive Man adapted to his environment and was sometimes changed by it. Today, Modern Man's environment includes a fantastic array of commercial products and services that must, in time, have their effect on the millions who use them. Carrying this premise to its ridiculous extreme, here is how we at MAD envision:

The Long Range Effects Of Products On People

ARTIST: JACK RICKARD

WRITER: DON REILLY

Wildroot Cream Head

Prolonged application of various chemicals to make hair manageable will result in a decalcifying of the skull, making the head itself soft and floppy and easy to manage.

131

Bell's Ear

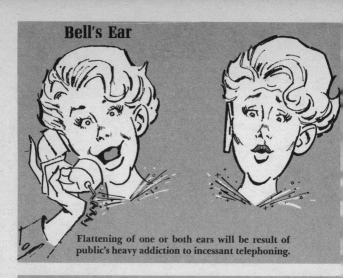

Flattening of one or both ears will be result of public's heavy addiction to incessant telephoning.

Compact Cramp

Years of squeezing and squashing into gnome-tailored foreign and domestic economy autos will result in a severe loss of limb-joint mobility and flexibility

Stretch-Pants Stance

Spindly look will result from prolonged use of tight stretch pants, compressing muscles, flesh and bones into atrophied masses of what were once legs and hips.

Aerosol Index Finger

Increased application of pressure-can-packing will result in over-development of the activating digit.

Twist-Off Triceps

Long-range outcome of housewives' daily struggle with them easy, twist-off tops.

Wallet Waddle

Permanent limp caused by years of lugging around fat wallets stuffed with plastic credit cards, laundry slips, photos, money, etc.—all the items necessary in order for modern citizens to function in our society.

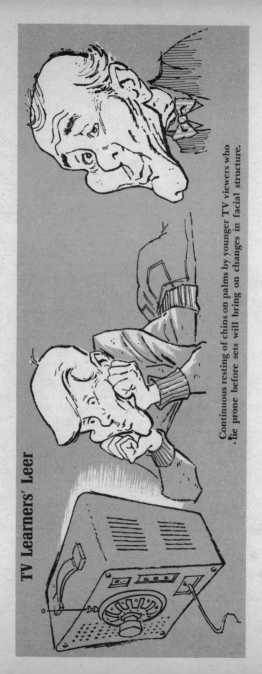

TV Learners' Leer

Continuous resting of chins on palms by younger TV viewers who lie prone before sets will bring on changes in facial structure.

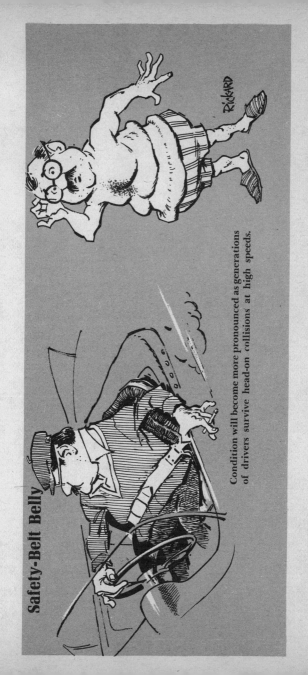

Safety-Belt Belly

Condition will become more pronounced as generations of drivers survive head-on collisions at high speeds.

Shutterbug Squint

Camera fanatics will develop permanent wink from incessant snap-snap-snapping.

Finger Feet

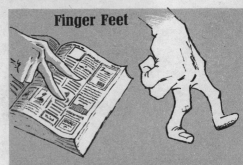

A physical result of generations of lazy slobs letting their fingers do the walking through *The Yellow Pages*

Filter Face

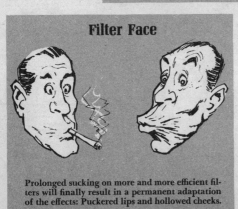

Prolonged sucking on more and more efficient filters will finally result in a permanent adaptation of the effects: Puckered lips and hollowed cheeks.

Housewives' Arm

Continuous stretching into top-loading automatic washers and deep freezes will cause this eventual physiological oddity: mainly the shorter the woman, the longer the arm.

Pop-Top Thumb

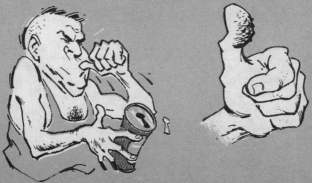

Layers of scar tissue will build up from constant cutting on fiendish pop-top cans.

141

Dave Berg once coached a Little League team, so he knows something about the subject. He may even agree with the critics of this Junior Sport who say, "Get the parents out of Little League and give it back to the kids!" Certainly all the players on the Little League team Dave coached will agree! They lost every game!

THE LIGHTER SIDE OF

What's the run-down on **adult leadership** on a little league team?

Well, let's see! There's one team manager . . . two team coaches . . .

and EIGHTY THIRD BASE COACHES!

little
league

WRITER & ARTIST: DAVID BERG

143

145

Al Buffington, ol' boy! That's **your son** up there at bat! Now let's try not to act like those **other** over-emotional parents who so **strongly identify** with their children that they make **fools** of themselves whenever their kids get up to the plate!

Pretend to be **nonchalant!** Show **no emotion!** Don't let anyone see how you're **dying** inside because there are **two strikes** on your boy!!

THANK GOODNESS!! HE GOT A HIT!

Watch it, Mr. Buffington! Remember . . . **no emotion!!**

I must say, Al ol' boy, you carried that off **rather well!!**

149

How come my son is only a **substitute**? Are you afraid he's going to show up **your** son? Aren't you showing **prejudice?** My son should be the **star pitcher!!**

Your boy pitches **very well** for his age! His curve ball **really curves,** and his slow ball actually seems to **hang in mid-air!** The trouble is, no one can hit his pitches!

SEE!? SEE!? YOU ADMIT IT YOURSELF! IF NO ONE CAN HIT HIS PITCHES, WHY DON'T YOU LET HIM PITCH?

Because his pitches **still don't reach home plate!**

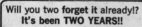

154

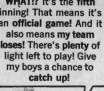

Hold it! I'm calling this game on account of darkness!

WHAT!? It's the **fifth** inning! That means it's an **official game!** And it also means my **team loses!** There's **plenty** of light left to play! Give my boys a chance to **catch** up!

It's **dangerous** for kids to play when they **can't see** a pitched ball!

Who can't see a pitched ball! The **sun's** still shining!

G'wan. The sun set at 7:22—and it's **eight o'clock** now!

Eight o'clock? You're out of your ever-lovin' **mind!** Le'me see that watch . . .

Okay! So it's eight o'clock! I **still** say there's **plenty** of light left to play . . .

One of the most interesting species of wildlife found on the American scene is that strange creature known as "The Politician". He conveniently changes color to match his surroundings, he's friendly to his opponent's face—then attacks him when his back is turned, and he scratches for votes at election time—then hibernates for his term of office. Since "The Politician" is such a strange creature who speaks a strange language, we present a simple primer to help explain him to you when he appears again during this campaign year.

THE MAD POLITICIAN'S PRIMER

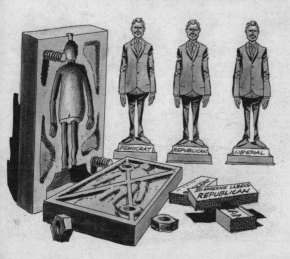

ARTIST: GEORGE WOODBRIDGE

WRITER: STAN HART

Lesson 1.

THE OFFICE SEEKER

See the politician.
He is making an announcement.
It is three months before elections.
He is announcing that he is not a candidate.
The timing is very important.
He must announce that he is not a candidate
Before the opposing candidate
Announces that *he* is not a candidate.

See the politician talking to the Party big shots.
He is talking to them about the nomination.
In politics, this is known as "sampling opinion".
Outside of politics, this is known as "begging".
The Party big shots ask him about foreign policy.
The Party big shots ask him about domestic policy.
The Party big shots ask him about economic policy.
The Party big shots ask him if he wants the nomination.
The politician answers "Yes!".
They have finally asked him a question he can answer.

Lesson 2.
THE CANDIDATE

See the popular candidate.
See him say, "Some of my best friends are Italian,
And Irish,
And German, and Polish, and Puerto Rican."
The candidate has no Gypsy friends.
There is no Gypsy vote.

The candidate is very interested in charity work.
He has been Chairman of Protestant Relief,
Catholic Charities, and United Jewish Appeal . . .
All at the same time.
Every four years, he hates discrimination.
See his liberal, open-minded family.
See them mingle with everyone.
See if you can spot the candidate's daughter.
You can't. She isn't here.
That's because she has been disinherited—
She married outside her religion.

Lesson 3.

THE CANDIDATE'S FAMILY

See the candidate with his wife.
She is so happy.
It's the fiirst time he's taken her out in 4 years.
If he wins the election
She will go to Washington.
If he loses the election
She will go back in the closet.
She is a dedicated woman.
She stands by him in city after city.
She doesn't trust him out of her sight.
See the candidate's children posing for pictures.
They are very photogenic.
They are also very stupid.
They haven't been in school since the campaign started.

Lesson 4.

THE POLL

See the busy man.
He is working on a pre-election poll.
It is easy to check the accuracy of the poll.
If his candidate is ahead,
The poll is very scientific.
If his candidate is behind,
He feeds the results into a big machine.
The machine is called a garbage disposal unit.

The pollster questions a select group.
This is known as a representative sample.
Are you now, or have you ever been a representative sample?
Do you know anyone who has ever been a representative sample?
We do.
The candidate. His mother. His barber. His bookie . . .

Lesson 5.

THE PUBLICITY MEN

See the publicity men.
They will give the candidate a new image.
They will teach him how to talk.
They will teach him how to smile.
They will make him popular.
If he doesn't get elected Congressman,
He might get elected "Miss Rheingold".

The publicity men take his picture wherever he goes.
And wherever he goes, the candidate eats.
One picture of him eating is worth a thousand words.
He eats a hot dog,
And it means "I am a typical American".
He eats a knish,
And it means "We are all God's children".
He eats a pizza,
And it means "Each minority group has contributed
     to make our country great".
The candidate needs a strong stomach to run for office.
Almost as strong a stomach as the people who vote for him.

Lesson 6.

THE CAMPAIGN CONTRIBUTION

See the rich man.
He contributes to the campaign fund.
He likes the candidate's platform.
The rich man is against giving government
　　　money to education.
The rich man is against giving government
　　　money to senior citizens.
The rich man is for "free enterprise".
Which means he's *for* giving government
　　　money to his missile factory.

The rich man owns many other things
Beside his missiles factory:
50 supermarkets, 10 liquor stores,
And a chain of department stores.
But he is not satisfied.
He has a dream.
This year his dream will come true.
He will own a Congressman.

Lesson 7.

THE CAMPAIGN TEAM

See the loyal campaign workers.
Half of them dig up damaging facts
About the candidate's opponent.
The other half do a more creative job:
They *manufacture* damaging facts
About the candidate's opponent.

The candidate has promised each campaign worker
That he is on a winning team.
The candidate has also promised each campaign worker
That he will be the next Ambassador to England.
Actually, the Ambassador will be
Someone who is distinguished,
Someone who is dependable,
Someone who is mature,
Someone who is the candidate's uncle.

Lesson 8.

THE CAMPAIGN SPEECH

Listen to the candidate making a speech.
Ask him a question.
He will say, "I'm glad you asked that question."
Aren't you glad *you* asked that question?
Wouldn't you be even gladder
If he *answered* that question?

When the candidate talks to Union groups,
He criticizes Management.
When he talks to Management groups,
He criticizes Unions.
At mixed rallies,
He develops laryngitis.

Lesson 9.

THE CAMPAIGN

See the unhappy candidate.
He has just been smeared by his opponents.
They have used dirty tactics.
They have said terrible things.
They have just recited his past record in Congress.

They claim he took six trips to Europe.
He claims they were Government business—
Like his official tour of NATO installations on the Riviera.
To get the woman's point of view,
He took along his pretty secretary.
His opponents ask what he has done for his constituents.
They claim he has been absent from Congress 90% of the time.
Probably that is the best thing he has done for his constituents.

The other day, we came upon a small boy sitting on a curb, reading **The New York Times,** and crying. "Why are you crying, little boy?" we asked. "Because," he sobbed, "there ain't no comics in this newspaper!" This started us thinking. Practically everybody loves comics — and yet there are lots of publications that don't run them! How awful! How deplorable! But mainly, how wonderful! Because it gives us this opportunity to fill up four ridiculous pages with these:

COMICS
FOR
PUBLICATIONS
THAT
DON'T
HAVE
COMICS

ARTIST: BOB CLARKE   WRITER: FRANK JACOBS

177

178

179

DADDY-O — for Variety

187

COOKIE THE BOOKIE
— for The Morning Telegraph

"Okay, Jimmy! You've bet three popsicles on Flying Flash to win! Marvin, I've got you down for six bubble-gum cards on Rose Petal to place! Sorry, Eddie, but I'm not taking any frogs, unless they're alive! If ya wanna bet on Dish Water, ya gotta put up something valuable, like an alarm clock spring . . . or your baby sister!